M000216095

**Learn REST APIs**

2nd Edition

Adonis Gaitatzis

BackupBrain Publishing, 2019

ISBN: 978-1-989775-00-4

backupbrain.co

**Learn REST APIs**

by Tony Gaitatzis

*To Nick and Chrisoula, for all the fresh tea*

# Table of Contents

# Introduction

The Internet runs on APIs. Social media apps, hotel, and travel sites, Netflix, and more use APIs to load, save, and analyze data over the Internet.

APIs or "Application Programming Interfaces" are computer programs that talk to other computer programs. They provide an interface for programmed applications to communicate, and they are becoming big business.

Representational State Transfer or REST APIs are a type of API hosted by a Web server, typically selling or analyzing data for customers via the web. These data analysis tools are built so that they can be used by 3rd party products such as mobile apps and other web sites. They enable companies to create new revenue streams at near-zero cost by monetizing their existing services. To a business, a REST API is like a white-label product or service they can offer to clients.

Some companies that offer APIs include:

- Google Maps,

- SalesForce,

- Amazon,

- Twitter, and

- Yahoo! Finance.

Many other companies use APIs internally to streamline development on multiple platforms such as iPhone, Android, and Desktop. For example, Facebook and LinkedIn use APIs so that their engineers have access to the same data regardless of what platform they are programming for. That way, deploying upgrades is much easier because the majority of changes are centralized in the API instead of numerous platforms.

APIs also allow for a snappier, more interactive user experience. Instead of loading everything upfront, an app or website can download important content on startup, then passively download only necessary content from APIs as a user interacts with the user interface, such as by scrolling and clicking on buttons and links.

For example, when scrolling through news headlines on a blog or news site that seems to have never-ending content. The news site queries an API for ten or twenty headlines when the site loads. As the user scrolls down, the site queries the API again for another ten or twenty headlines, inserting them at the end of the page and allowing the user to continue scrolling. Each time the user nears the bottom of the page, the site queries the API again and inserts more content, making the website content seem endless.

REST APIs allow for faster development cycles, faster and more interactive software products, and better separation of content and presentation on any platform.

When correctly implemented, REST APIs are highly standardized, so much so that most modern software can read and write data to REST

APIs out of the box, allowing developers to focus on how to best use the data rather than how to connect, authenticate, and download it. When correctly implemented and documented, it can create a practically free passive revenue stream by monetizing a company's existing work.

# 1

---

## Introduction to REST APIs

---

### What is a REST API?

REST APIs are a standard way of providing access to data from a web server to clients such as mobile apps, web sites, or Internet of Things devices. They can allow clients to create, remove, update, or delete data, or to provide some type of data analysis.

Typically, people do not interact with REST APIs directly. Instead, people interact with client software on their phone, browser, or another device, which in turn requests and modifies data from one or more REST APIs in the background.

REST API is typically programmed with a web scripting language such as Python, Ruby on Rails, or PHP, which interacts with a database or other APIs. The REST API is accessible by URL, just like a website. Except instead of requesting a website with a web browser, another software client is requesting data. The scripting language is configured to run through a web server such as Apache or NGINX so that requests can be processed and responses can be delivered back to the client via the Internet. When a client submits a request via a URL, the server determines what action to take and how to process and present any data involved. It responds with a status code, some formatting headers, and structured data.

The client retrieves this data and converts it into something useful to the program or its users. The server treats each request as a new, unique request, meaning it does not store session variables or maintain any state information about the client. A REST API may have many clients and a client talk to many REST APIs. The software that powers a REST API may also be a client for other REST APIs.

The data stored on a REST server is called a *resource*. This can be any type of data, from time-sensitive data such as stock quotes, real-world data such as contact information, documents, images, audio, or anything else. In some cases, the actual resource data is stored in a database on the server, but with REST this resource is typically represented in JSON, XML, or some other common format that is compatible with HTTP. JSON is the most popular.

The same resource can be represented in either JSON or XML, for example details of the book "War and Peace" by Leo Tolstoy represented in JSON:

```
{
  "title": "War and Peace",
  "author": "Leo Tolstoy",
  "published_year": "1869",
  "num_pages": "1225"
}
```

*Example 2.1: Details of the book "War and Peace" represented in JSON*

The same book resource represented in XML:

```
<root>
  <book>
    <title>War and Peace</title>
    <author>Leo Tolstoy</author>
    <published_year>1869</published_year>
    <num_pages>1225</num_pages>
  </book>
</root>
```

*Example 2.2: Details of the book "War and Peace" represented in XML*

More information about the JSON data format can be found at http://json.org.

Using a common representation and the REST protocol, a client can access or modify a resource using a REST interface. Many REST APIs exist to perform a variety of tasks, from payment processing, marketing, finance, travel and logistics, sports, weather, and more.

A few interesting APIs include:

- **Stripe** (stripe.com): allows developers to integrate credit card processing into their website so they can create an online store.

- **From Data With Love** (fromdatawithlove.com): predicts demographic information based on people's name and job title.

- **SkyScanner** (skyscanner.com) provides flight prices and route tracking information.

- **OpenWeatherMap** (openweathermap.org) provides historical and current, and forecasted weather data.

- **Yahoo! Finance** (yahoo.com) provides stock quotes.

- **DataDemograph** (datademograph.com) provides demographic information for US addresses.

- **Yelp** (yelp.com) provides photos, menus, reviews, and hours of operations for restaurants.

- **Rebrandly** (rebrandly.com) creates custom tiny URLs.

## Who Uses REST APIs?

Although REST is typically human-readable, it is designed to be used by other software known as a Client. REST APIs are made so that other software developers can add functionality to their software and apps. REST services are client-agnostic, meaning that any type of client software can interface with them. A web browser, a smartphone, a smartwatch, or any other software can interface with a REST server. The REST server does not know or care what type of client connects.

The REST API provides representations of resources, which can be used or displayed in any way the client sees fit. For example, FlightAware has a flight tracker API. Using this API, flight alert and tracker clients have been built for iPhone, Android, smartwatches, web browsers, and email clients to name a few. Any technology that can connect to the Internet and talk to an HTTP server can become a REST client.

For example, here are just a few clients that use the FlightAware API.

*Figure 2.2: Screen captures of flight tracking API clients*

What makes REST APIs useful then is that they provide easy access to useful data so that other developers can create better applications with richer data in less time. In providing this, a REST API can make money by charging small amounts of money for many applications to access data simultaneously. For this reason, most REST APIs restrict who can access what data, what permissions are granted, and how many requests can be made in some period of time.

## How do REST APIs Work?

REST APIs power all modern apps and websites. They are a protocol, a way of doing things rather than a specific programming language or technology. REST APIs generally provide a predictable mechanism to let a client take one or more actions with structured data at one or more endpoints.

The REST protocol requires that each function is accessible via a unique URL or Endpoint. HTTP methods represent actions, each endpoint represents a unique resource type, and structured data represents the resource.

In a traditional website, a user navigates their browser to a unique website address known as a Uniform Resource Locator or URL. The user's browser downloads content and supporting files, typically HTML, JavaScript, images, and stylesheets from the web server at this address and renders them as a web page. Each link a user clicks on the web page causes the browser to access another web page URL and supporting files. Each page load is static and stateless, meaning that each page can be loaded independently. Forms can be used to add or alter a user's data in the web application and altered user content can only be displayed when a new page is loaded. This paradigm provides slow user experience and is resource-intensive for both the server and the browser.

By loading data from URLs in the background, REST APIs allow web applications to update without rendering a whole new page. The resulting mobile apps and websites allow users to interactively modify their data across the Internet, without having to load a new page and supporting files. When well done, the result is websites that load and render in a few seconds and provide app-like interaction using content provided by potentially many data providers. This paradigm allows for faster development cycles on a broader number of platforms, a faster user experience, reduced server load, and unlimited interaction.

An example of this is Facebook. Facebook provides APIs for its applications so that both the mobile apps and website access the same content and so the mobile apps and website behave like the same interactive application. Facebook's APIs allow these apps to send and display status updates, images, comments, reactions, and messages.

REST doesn't create or modify data. It is the format that allows client and server software to talk to each other. Both client and server software may create or modify data, but the common language they use to communicate is REST.

# 2

---

# Understanding HTTP

---

## How REST Relates to HTTP

Before understanding REST, it is important to understand HTTP.

REST APIs typically work over the HyperText Transfer Protocol (HTTP), a protocol used for transmitting data on the World Wide Web. HTTP is what web browsers use to download web pages and to submit web forms. Whenever a person uses a web browser, that browser uses HTTP to ask a web server to access some data from a web site. HTTP also forms the transportation layer of REST APIs. Except instead of a person downloading a web site with a browser, a software client accesses data from a server via a REST API.

HTTP provides a convenient way of packaging data so that it contains useful information about how that data is intended to be used.

## HTTP Request and Response

HTTP is a client/server architecture, meaning that clients mostly request and update data to a server, which acts as a central repository for the data. The server is responsible for storing and saving changes, as well as responding to requests to access data by the clients. Each request by a client triggers a response by the server.

The client makes requests and the server responds, like this:

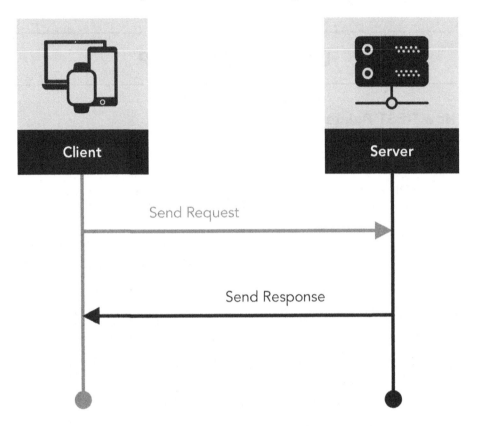

*Figure 3.1: Request and response interaction between client and server*

Any time a client makes an HTTP request to an API server, the server interprets and processes the request and returns a response with information about how the request was interpreted and processed or what the resulting resource looks like.

## Anatomy of an HTTP Request

When a REST client makes a request or the server responds, a data package of all these elements is assembled using the HTTP protocol and sent across the Internet.

The HTTP Request has four parts. A method, a URI, headers, and a payload. The method describes what action must be taken with any data that may be included in the request. The URI locates the resource the client wants to access. The payload consists of any data that is to be sent to the server, and headers describe the nature of that payload data.

The data package looks like this:

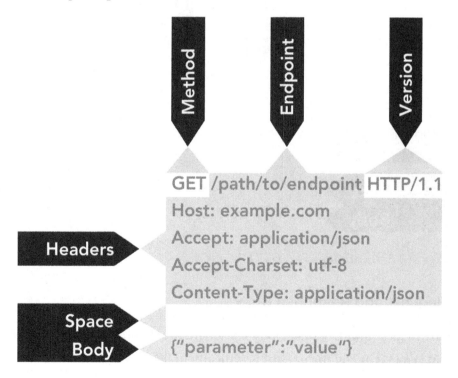

*Figure 3.2: Anatomy of an HTTP request*

## Anatomy of an HTTP Response

When a REST server responds to a client's request, a data package of all these elements is assembled using the HTTP protocol and sent across the Internet back to the client.

The data package looks like this:

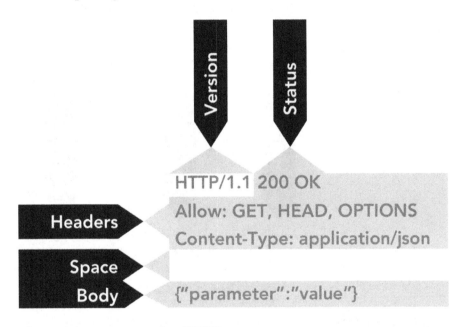

*Figure 3.3: Anatomy of an HTTP response*

## Request and Response Body

The request and response body are where the REST data goes. This data can be in any format but is typically in JSON. Other formats might include XML for relational or tabular data, HTML for rich text, binary for movies, pictures, and video, or text. Sometimes this data is gzipped or encrypted.

## HTTP Headers

HTTP supports customizable headers, which each contain important information about the resource data and its format. This information typically includes metadata about how long the data is relevant for, what format the data is in, or other information such as authorization keys or encryption type. Headers are sent in both the request and response, and since the headers relate to the data being sent, they are unique to each request and to each response.

Typical HTTP headers for REST requests include:

| Header | Description | Example |
|---|---|---|
| Authorization | The client's authorization credentials | BASIC VGhpcyBpcyBhIHR lc3Q= |
| Content-Length | The length of the data in bytes | 1923 |
| Content-MD5 | An MD5 hash of the data | d4a654c273edaea1b 01254df9a1201f3 |
| Accept | The MIME-type expected by the client | application/json |

| | | |
|---|---|---|
| Accept-Charset | The text encoing expected by the client | utf-8 |

*Table 3.1: Common HTTP headers used in REST API requests*

A full list of HTTP request headers can be found in *Appendix I: HTTP Request Headers*.

Typical HTTP headers for REST responses include:

| Header | Description | Example |
|--------|-------------|---------|
| Content-Type | The data format and text encoding being sent | application/json; charset=utf-8 |
| Expires | The expiration date of the data | Tue, 15 Nov 1994 08:12:31 GMT |
| Access-Control-Allow-Origin | Website domains that are allowed use this URI | example.com,* |
| Access-Control-Allow-Methods | Verbs that are supported by this URI by remote clients | OPTIONS,GET,PUT |
| Allow | Verbs that are supported by this URI locally | OPTIONS,GET,PUT |
| Content-Encoding | Is the content compressed | gzip |
| Content-Language | The natural language of the data | en |
| Content-Length | The length of the data in bytes | 1923 |
| Content-MD5 | An MD5 hash of the data | d4a654c273edaea1b 01254df9a1201f3 |
| Cache-Control | A description of the cacheing rules for clients | private, no-cache, must-revalidate |

*Table 3.2: Common HTTP headers used in REST API responses*

A full list of HTTP response headers can be found in *Appendix II: HTTP Response Headers.*

## Uniform Resource Identifiers

A Uniform Resource Identifiers (URI) is a way of providing standardized addresses for resources on the World Wide Web. This addressing scheme has a particular syntax that guarantees each website domain will provide a standard, uniquely identifiable way of accessing its resources.

The anatomy of a URI is as follows:

| Protocol | Website Domain | Resource path |
|---|---|---|
| https:// | example.com | /path/to/index.html |

*Table 3.2: Parts of a URI*

## HTTP Request Methods

When a client makes a request to a server, it must tell the server what action it wants the server to take with some data. HTTP has several possible methods that allow a client to create, read, update, or delete data. These four operations are so important that they are known by an acronym, *CRUD*. In REST, these actions are known as *verbs*.

| Verb | HTTP Method |
| --- | --- |
| Create | POST |
| Read | GET |
| Update | PUT |
| Append | PATCH |
| Delete | DELETE |
| Endpoint Documentation | OPTIONS |
| Access HTTP Headers Only | HEAD |

*Table 3.3: HTTP request methods*

With these verbs, it is possible to program a REST API that allows users to create, read, update, and delete data. Additionally, several methods exist to inspect documentation for an endpoint and what level of access a client has to that endpoint.

When browsing the web, GET is the default HTTP method. It asks to get data from the web server. When submitting a form on a website from a browser, the website typically submits the form using the POST Method. This tells the web server to add new data to the server's program with data found in the HTTP body.

Because REST is all about data manipulation, each of these verbs may be available to perform relevant CRUD operations.

## GET

A REST client will read a resource using a `GET` request to an endpoint. This request may include login credentials. If the request was processed properly, the server's response will include the `Content-Type` header with a MIME-type description of the data format, plus a resource with the corresponding data format. JSON is the most common REST data format. In such cases, the `Content-Type` header is set to `application/json` and the response is represented in JSON.

## POST

A client sends a resource using a `POST` request to create a new resource on the server. The request must set the `Content-Type` MIME-type to the same data format as the resource format. If the resource is successfully created by the server, good REST API will return the ID of the newly created resource in its response body.

After this transaction, any client in the world with access to this resource can access it using a GET request.

## PUT

PUT is used to alter or replace an existing resource. The PUT request
and response is formatted the same way as the POST request, with
JSON or other data format and a corresponding MIME-type in
the Content-Type header.

After this transaction, any client in the world with access to this
resource can access the updated resource using a GET request.

## PATCH

PATH is used to append data to an existing resource without replacing
it. The request and response are formatted just like in PUT and POST,
with JSON or other data format and a corresponding MIME-type in
the Content-Type header.

After this transaction, any client in the world with access to this
resource can access the updated resource using a GET request.

## DELETE

DELETE is used to delete a resource. Typically it is impossible to delete
multiple resources at once. Typically no resource is sent in the request
body. Once the transaction is complete, clients no longer have access
to this resource.

## OPTIONS

OPTIONS used by web browsers that verify permissions in the browser
before making a full API request. It is critical to implement in a full
REST API. This method will return a header with a comma-separated

list of allowed HTTP methods as well as other permission and caching information, such as this:

```
Cache-Control: private, no-cache, must-revalidate
Expires: Tue, 15 Nov 1994 08:12:31 GMT
Allow: OPTIONS,GET,PUT
Access-Control-Allow-Methods: OPTIONS,GET,PUT
```

*Example 3.3: Example HTTP OPTION response headers*

## HEAD

HEAD shows just the HTTP headers for the response, for example:

```
200 OK
Content-Type: application/json; encoding=utf-8
Allow: OPTIONS,GET,PUT
Access-Control-Allow-Methods: OPTIONS,GET,PUT
```

*Example 3.4: Example HTTP HEAD response headers*

## Response Status Codes

When a server responds to a request, it must inform the client of the status of the request. Sometimes a request is executed properly and sometimes it fails for some reason. Sometimes payment is required or the client doesn't have sufficient privileges to perform the request. This part of the response is given as a numeric code.

A typical REST response will have a 200 OK response code, meaning that the request was interpreted properly and the data was delivered. A 404 Not Found response code will be returned if the client requests an invalid URI, the same response code that is returned when a person follows a dead link on a web page.

Status Codes commonly associated with REST APIs include:

| Code | Name | Description |
| --- | --- | --- |
| 200 | OK | Default - Request was executed successfully |
| 201 | Created | New data was inserted |
| 202 | Accepted | The request was processed successfully, data has been modified on the server |
| 204 | No Content | Request was executed successfully but no resource was returned |
| 301 | Moved Permanently | This URI has been moved |
| 305 | Not Modified | No action was taken. Typically used with cached URIs |
| 400 | Bad Request | This URI is not active |
| 401 | Unauthorized | The client must log in to access this URI |
| 403 | Forbidden | The client does not have sufficient permissions to access this URI |
| 404 | Not Found | This URI is not active |

| Code | Name | Description |
|------|------|-------------|
| 405 | Method Not Allowed | This verb is not active for this URI |
| 429 | Too Many Requests | The client has accessed the API or URI too many times in some amount of time |
| 500 | Internal Server Error | The server encountered a bug |

*Table 3.4: HTTP response status codes commonly used in REST APIs*

As the server attempts to process the request and deliver the response, any number of problems may occur. The sequence of potential problems is as follows:

# Understanding HTTP

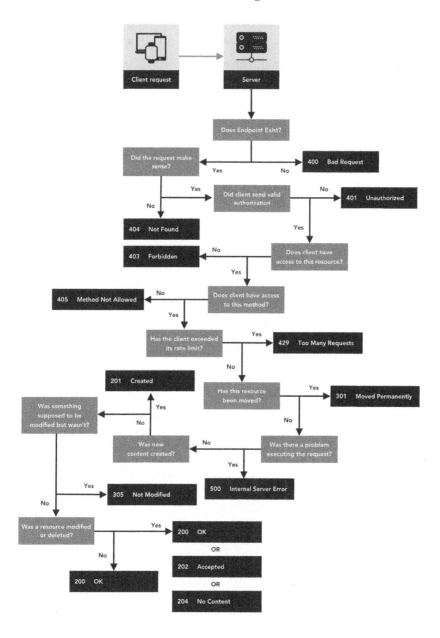

*Figure 3.4: Possible request / response interactions*

Generally speaking, Status Codes 200-299 indicate a successful operation. 300-399 indicate that the endpoint has moved. 400-499 indicate that the client did something wrong, resulting in an error. 500-599 indicate that an error was encountered on the server.

# 3

---

## Understanding REST

---

REST, or Representational State Transfer refers to a type of software architecture principles that result in efficient, reliable systems that scale well. The six REST principles are:

1. Client/Server Architecture

2. Statelessness

3. Cacheability

4. Layered Platform Agnosticism

5. Code on Command

6. Uniform, predictable interface

Deviating from any of these principles makes an API not a REST API. Developers are often implicitly trained on these principles when working with REST APIs and most web-enabled software is programmed to work with REST. Therefore any deviation from these principles will not only limit scalability, reliability, and efficiency but will also make it more difficult for developers to learn and debug and could possibly break compatibility with other REST-compatible software.

## Client/Server Architecture

REST is implemented on both the client and the server. The client manages the user interface and the server manages data storage and heavy processing. This ensures a clean division of roles.

The result is a highly portable system where a single REST service can deliver the same quality of service to any type of client without knowing how the client presents the result to the user. As a result of this design, a single API such as the Twitter API can display the same tweets on a desktop browser, a smartphone, a smartwatch, or any other system.

## Statelessness

REST APIs cannot rely on the client context or state information to operate. The REST API must not know between requests if the user is logged in, what previous API calls they have made, or anything else. The client is responsible for keeping track of its own session state, and all API requests must be treated as a one-off request.

A session state must be sent as part of the request if it is necessary or relevant. For example, it is common to require a client to log in prior to accessing a REST API. In cases like these, often the client either sends the login credentials with each request or requests a session token in a login request, then sends that session token with each subsequent request.

## Cacheability

Caching, or saving responses for some period of time is a common performance optimization in REST APIs. However, all REST responses must be accurately defined in the HTTP header as cacheable or non-cacheable to ensure the client works as expected. Caching responses that are unlikely to change, responses that are expected to change periodically, and content that is expected to change constantly all must be given proper caching headers in order to function properly.

For example, if an endpoint delivers fresh content with every request, the response will include the following HTTP header:

```
Cache-Control: private, no-cache, must-revalidate
```

*Example 4.1: HTTP Header for non-cacheable content*

If an endpoint will refresh its content on January 1st, 2050, the response will include the following HTTP header:

```
Expires: Sat, 1 Jan 2050 01:00:00 GMT
```

*Example 4.2: HTTP Header for content that must be cached until January 1, 2050*

If an endpoint expects data to be valid for 24 hours (86400 seconds) from the last request, the response might include the following HTTP header:

```
Cache-Control: private, max-age=86400
```

*Example 4.3: HTTP Header for content that must be cached for 24 hours*

These headers tell the client when the server is likely to provide updated data about a resource. If a client accesses an endpoint while the data is cached, it will likely get the same response from the server and will burn one more request. This may be important not only for efficiency and scale but also since many APIs charge money for a limited number of requests.

## Layered Platform Agnosticism

The system must be designed so the client can't know and doesn't care if it is connected directly to a server or an intermediary system such as a Content Delivery Network (CDN), caching server, a proxy, or a mirror. This ensures scalability and security. It also ensures reliability when upgrading or replacing servers.

The system must also not care what technology powers the client or the server. A REST API must deliver the same service to an Apple Watch as it does to a web application. A web application or Apple Watch must be able to communicate with a REST API written in Ruby on Rails, Python, PHP, or anything else regardless of what language it uses internally.

## Code on Command

REST Servers can transfer executable code such as client-side
JavaScript or pre-compiled components to the client to extend and
customize functionality. Though rarely used, this feature must be
supported in order to have a RESTful API. This just means that a
REST server might transmit code, byte-code, or binary as a resource
and that a client of such an API would be expected to execute that
code.

## Uniform, Predictable Architecture

REST must have a uniform interface, meaning that it must be written
and behave the same way at all times, at all places in the API. This
ensures ease of adoption, predictability, scalability, and efficiency.

REST has four components which must be considered when
discussing uniformity and predictability. These are:

1.  Endpoints and URIs

2.  Representation Manipulation

3.  A consistent interface must be used to describe messages and
    data.

4.  Hyperlinks must be used to describe the location of other
    resources and methods.

## Endpoints and URIs

An endpoint is the address of a resource. Since REST APIs exist on the Internet, this address is a file path on a web server. It uses nouns to describes what resource the client is requesting. So a contact-management API that lets a user access contact information for a person might have an endpoint like `/person/john_doe` and not `/get_person/john_doe`. A finance API that lets users access stock prices might have an endpoint for the Netflix stock at `/stocks/NASDAQ/NFLX` and not `/search/nasdaq_stocks?stock=NFLX`.

The URI, or Uniform Resource Identifier is used on the web to send a request. The URI combines the domain name of the REST API, for example, `http://api.example.com` and the API endpoint to create an address that is unique and available on the Internet.

For example, if `example.com` provides an API for historical weather data by city and date, an API endpoint might be `/weather/`. A client might want to access weather from the city of `London` in the `UK` on the date `2019-06-19`. The weather data for this place and date is a resource.

A unique URI must be constructed to request this resource, which might resemble this:

`https://api.example.com/1.0/weather/UK/London/2019-06-19`

*Example 4.4: URI for a London weather endpoint hosted by api.example.com*

Additional query parameters may be added to the request to customize the response. For instance, perhaps this service supports returning the temperatures in metric or imperial units with the units parameter.

REST URIs come in a specific format, making it easy to predict what such a URI would look like:

| | |
|---|---|
| **Protocol** | https:// |
| **Domain** | api.example.com |
| **Version** | 1.0 |
| **API Endpoint** | /weather/ |
| **Entity** | UK/London |
| **Record** | 2019-06-19 |
| **Parameters** | ?units=metric |

*Table 4.1: REST Endpoint and URI construction.*

In the URI, any data set, record, or filter is named by nouns such as weather, London, or calendar date.

## Representation Manipulation

Given adequate permissions, any client must be able to create, modify, update, or delete a resource. Additionally, a *preview* verb must be supported to allow web clients to check permissions of a resource.

These actions are accessed using the following HTTP verbs:

| Action | HTTP Verb | Notes |
|---|---|---|
| Create | POST | Optional |
| Read | GET | Optional but common |
| Update | PUT | Optional |
| Delete | DELETE | Optional |
| Preview Documentation | OPTIONS | Required |
| Get Headers | HEAD | Required |

*Table 4.2: Relationship between HTTP methods and REST verbs.*

These verbs are necessary to perform transactions in HTTP. By default, a web browser assumes a GET operation, since most of web browsing is only reading content. Since REST is about data, most implement all six verbs. Minimally, any endpoint must support OPTIONS and HEAD, plus another depending on the function the endpoint performs. For example, an endpoint that only allows a client to read a resource must support GET, OPTIONS, and HEAD. An endpoint that only lets a client create new resources must support POST,

OPTIONS, and HEAD. An endpoint that lets a client create, read, and alter resources must support GET, POST, PUT, OPTIONS, and HEAD.

## Consistent Interface Between Messages and Data

A consistent interface must be used to describe messages and data. This means that the headers must accurately describe the properties of the data in the body. The Content-Type header must be included with every request and response and must describe the encoding and format using a MIME-type. MIME-types are a standard way of describing data formats on the Internet. They describe both the type and format of data.

Some common REST data formats and corresponding MIME-types include:

| Data Format | MIME-type |
|---|---|
| JSON | application/json |
| XML | application/xml |
| text | text/plain |
| HTML | text/html |
| PNG Image | image/png |
| JPG Image | image/jpeg |
| MP3 Audio | audio/mpeg3 |
| MPEG Video | video/mpeg |

*Table 4.3: Common data types and corresponding MIME-types on the Internet.*

A full list of MIME-types can be found in *Appendix V: MIME Types*.

In the case of text and text data formats such as `text/plain`, `text/html`, `application/json`, and `application/xml`, the text encoding must be declared also. Common text encodings include UTF-8 and ISO-8859-1 (also known as ASCII). If the wrong encoding is used, it can be impossible to decipher the text properly, especially if it contains non-Latin characters or emojis. Over 90% of REST APIs use UTF-8 to encode text data, with ISO-8859-1 trailing at around 3%.

Therefore if the data in the body is JSON-formatted and UTF-8 encoded, the Content-Type header must describe that:

```
PUT /path/to/endpoint
Content-Type: application/json; encoding=utf-8

{
    "parameter":"value"
}
```

*Example 4.5: UTF-8 encoded JSON response*

If the data in the body is XML-formatted and ASCII-encoded, the Content-Type header must describe that:

```
PUT /path/to/endpoint
Content-Type: application/xml; encoding=iso-8859-1

<root>
    <parameter>
        value
    </parameter>
</root>
```

*Example 4.6: ISO-8859-1 encoded XML response*

Similarly, all other included headers must accurately describe the data. If the data is gzipped, the Content-Encoding header must reflect that. The Content-Length must be the byte length of the data body and Content-MD5 must be a Base64-encoded MD5sum of that data.

For example, a response containing an empty JSON object, {} would have the following `Content-Length` and `Content-MD5` headers:

```
200 OK
Content-Type: application/json; encoding=utf-8
Content-Length: 2
Content-MD5: 99914b932bd37a50b983c5e7c90ae93b


{}
```

*Example 4.7: Empty JSON object with corresponding MD5 and content length described in HTTP headers.*

## Use of Hyperlinks

As REST is a Web resource, all references to other resources such as documentation, other API endpoints, or other resources must be referenced using URIs. When presenting an error message, rather than saying, "See our documentation," provide a hyperlink to the referenced documentation. Rather than simply listing the ID of relevant resource from another, list the URI of that resource.

In the weather API example, maybe it is helpful to provide the previous and next day forecast. In this case, the API might include the following JSON code.

```
{
    // other weather forecast data
    "previous_day": "http://example.com/1.0/UK/London/
2019-06-18",
    "next_day": "http://example.com/1.0/UK/London/
2019-06-20",
}
```

*Example 4.8: Use of hyperlinks in JSON resource*

# 4

---

## Using REST APIs

---

### Authorization and Authentication

Many REST APIs are subscription-based, meaning a client can only access an API by authenticating with a login and password or an API key associated with an account. In such cases, the documentation and/or user dashboard should provide the login and password or API keys required to access the API properly, as well as for instructions on how to implement the authentication.

The first step is for a person, typically a developer to set up an account with the operator of the REST API. For example, if using the Twitter API, a person must register a Twitter account and then activate the developer features to get API keys to use the Twitter API in their own software.

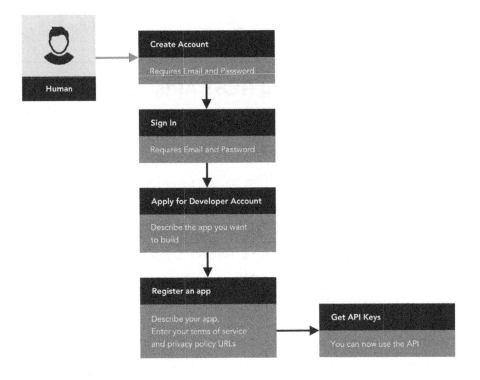

*Figure 5.1: Twitter's API key registration process*

Authorization is important to ensure that the developer uses the API
fairly. APIs typically enforce strict limits on how many requests can be
made in some period of time. These rate limits typically limit the
number of requests per month as a part of the subscription service
and limit the number of requests per minute to prevent
overwhelming the server. When a client exceeds its rate limit, the
server typically responds a 249 Too Many Requests status code and
an informative error message in the body of the response.

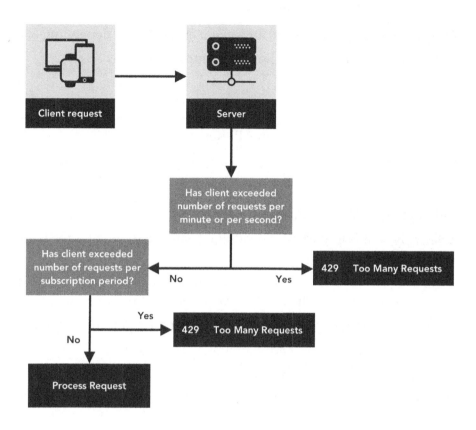

*Figure 5.2: Typical rate-limit logic*

Making an OPTIONS request endpoint will describe the permissions required to use the API, as well as descriptions and parameters for functions available at that endpoint. This documentation will be written in OpenAPI, RAML, Swagger, BluePrint, or some other markup language.

## API Keys and Login/Password

There are many possible ways for a client authenticate, depending on how the API is constructed. The most common methods are:

- An API Key

- Login and Password or an API Key and Secret in the header

- A Session Token

Although there are best practices, each API handles authentication differently so it is important to read the documentation to understand how to each one properly.

Many APIs require the client to submit authentication credentials with every request. requests that don't have proper authentication, or that access a restricted verb or endpoint will receive a 401 Unauthorized or 403 Forbidden response, possibly also with headers and data in the response body explaining the error or a link to the documentation.

Such a response looks like this:

```
401 Unauthorized
Content-Type: application/json; encoding=utf-8


{
    "error": "Login required",
    "description": "Create an account at http://
example.com and follow our login procedure in our API
documentation: http://docs.example.com/api/v1/"
}
```

*Example 5.6: Helpful response to unauthenticated client.*

When a client makes a request with proper authentication, the server will return a 200 OK and execute the function. If the client makes an OPTIONS request, the server will return a list of allowed verbs in the Access-Control-Allow-Methods and Allow HTTP headers, plus possibly some documentation in the response body. This is a typical interaction with web applications, where the browser verifies authentication before executing an intended API request.

Such a response might look like this:

```
200 OK
Content-Type: application/json; encoding=utf-8
Access-Control-Allow-Methods: GET, OPTIONS, HEAD
Allow: GET, OPTIONS, HEAD

"get": {
  "responses": {
    "200": {
```

```
      "description": "View a Superhero",
      "schema": {
        "$ref": "#/definitions/Superhero"
      }
    }
  }
}
```

*Example 5.7: Helpful response to an OPTIONS request of an authenticated client.*

Although some APIs expect the API key or login and password to be sent in the request body, most are sent in the HTTP Headers. Some have a custom header, such as X-Api-Key or X-Api-Authorization, but by far the most common method is to use the Authorization header provided by the HTTP specification.

The Authorization header supports several ways of encoding account information, BASIC, DIGEST, BEARER, or OAUTH. Typically, BASIC is used to encode a login and password or API key and secret. DIGEST is used to encode just an API key.

A table of example common REST Authorization schemes follows:

| Login | Password | Scheme | Encoding | Resulting Header |
|---|---|---|---|---|
| api_key | 1234 | BASIC | Base64 | BASIC YXBpX2tleTox MjM0 |
| api_key | (none) | DIGEST | Base64 | DIGEST YXBpX2tleQ= = |
| session _token | (none) | BEARER | None | BEARER session_token |
| session _token | (none) | OAUTH | None | OAUTH session_token |

*Table 5.1: Common authorization schemes used in REST*

In the case of BASIC Authorization, the login or API key is joined with the API secret or password with a colon (:) and Base64 encoded. This Base64 encoded string is preceded by the authentication scheme, for example BASIC or DIGEST. In either case, the client sends the resulting string in the Authorization HTTP header.

Most programming languages support Base64 encoding and there are several websites that will encode and decode Base64 text for free. One such website is base64decode.org.

If an API requires `DIGEST` encoding for an API key, a full API request might look like this:

```
GET /path/to/endpoint
Authorization: DIGEST YXBpX2tleQ==
```

*Example 5.8: Possible api_key authentication request using DIGEST scheme*

If an API requires BASIC encoding on login and password or an API key and secret, a full API request might look like this:

```
GET /path/to/endpoint
Authorization: BASIC YXBpX2tleToxMjM0
```

*Example 5.9: Possible username/password authentication request using BASIC scheme.*

Though common, these methods are insecure because Base64 is easily converted back into plain text. With Base64 encoding, the login and password or API key and secret are easy to read, especially if requests and responses aren't encrypted.

## Session Tokens and OAuth

API Servers that are more security-focused tend to use session tokens or OAuth authentication. This works by making a request to an authentication endpoint of the API with the login and password or API key and secret in the request body or in the header as described in the previous section. The server will return a time-sensitive, unique login token in either the header or the response body.

The client sends this API token with all subsequent requests in the request body or in the `Authorization` Header, typically with a `BEARER` or `OAUTH` scheme.

The basic workflow for this type of Authentication looks like this:

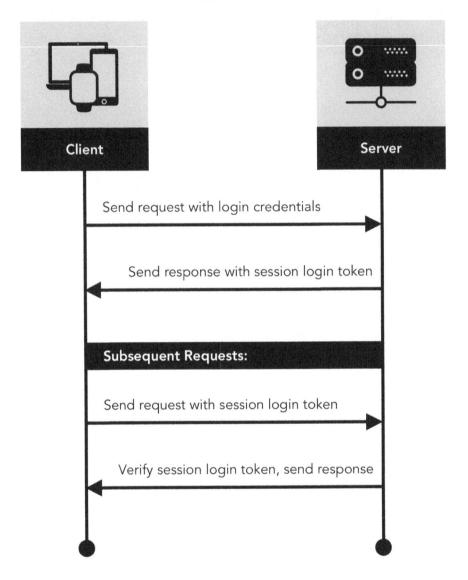

*Figure 5.4: Authorization and subsequent request workflow*

This process technically violates the stateless requirement of REST because it requires the server to maintain Session information for a client. Regardless, it is a compromise that dramatically enhances the security of an API because the login credentials are transmitted only once per session.

A fictional API that authenticates using session tokens from an /account/login endpoint might look like this:

The client makes a PUT request with the login credentials in the HTTP body.

```
PUT /account/login
Content-Type: application/json; encoding=utf-8

{"username": "api_key", "password": "1234"}
```

*Example 5.10: Possible api key and password authentication request using PUT method.*

The server sends a response with the session token in the HTTP body.

```
200 OK
Content-Type: application/json; encoding=utf-8

{"session_token": "5f4dcc3b5aa765d61d8327deb882cf99"}
```

*Example 5.11: Possible response from server containing a temporary login session token.*

The client send the authentication token in the Authorization header of subsequent requests. Typically the token is sent unencoded with a BEARER authentication scheme, like this:

```
GET /path/to/endpoint
Content-Type: application/json; encoding=utf-8
Authorization: BEARER 5f4dcc3b5aa765d61d8327deb882cf99
```

*Example 5.12: Possible subsequent requests using the session token as proof of login and the BEARER scheme*

Alternately, a server that supports OAuth authentication may require the login token to be sent with an OAUTH authentication scheme, like this:

```
GET /path/to/endpoint
Content-Type: application/json; encoding=utf-8
Authorization: OAUTH 5f4dcc3b5aa765d61d8327deb882cf99
```

*Example 5.12: Possible subsequent requests using the session token as proof of login and the OAUTH scheme*

Consult the documentation for each API regarding authentication as each API handles it differently.

## Finding New APIs

REST APIs can make your application more scalable, more reliable, more efficient, and can provide data and functions that would be impossible to provide in-house. But in order to use an API, you must find it.

Fortunately there are several API directories online. ProgrammableWeb (programmableweb.com), RapidAPI

(rapidapi.com), AnyAPI (any-api.com), Nordic APIs (nordicapis.com), and PublicAPIs (public-apis.xyz) are all such directories. Together these directories have over 50,000 APIs.

Additionally, there are API conferences such as API Conference (apiconference.net), API Days (apidays.com), and API:World (apiworld.com). At these conferences, it is possible to learn about the current state of API tools and best practices and to connect with many API vendors.

## Reading the Documentation

Using a REST API requires knowing how it works. Some APIs are simple, providing access to a simple algorithm or data with a single endpoint. Some are complex, providing many layers of permissions, hundreds of endpoints, and thousands of parameters. Some are so obvious that glancing at the API is enough to understand how it works, and some require extensive research and testing before being able to use them.

Fortunately, REST provides a standard for how to package and format data to an API server. This makes it possible to read and interpret how to make and receive requests. Good REST APIs have extensive, human-readable documentation with example requests and responses, and possibly error codes. This allows people to know what features an API provides and how to access them, how to know when something went wrong, and how to write code that best works with that API.

Additionally, many REST APIs provide a map of features in the response body when making an OPTIONS request. This will typically be presented in open-source formats such as OpenAPI, RAML, or Blueprint. This makes it possible to write software that determines the feature map of an API.

A lot of human-readable API documentation is also created using these formats and hosted on platforms such as Swagger (swagger.io) and Apiary (apiary.io).

OpenAPI and RAML are YAML-based languages, Swagger supports YAML and JSON, and BluePrint is Markdown-based. All these languages are designed to be both human-readable and code-friendly.

Take for example an API that lets users read the name, age, and superpower of a superhero. All resources are delivered in JSON notation and the client must supply a superhero ID to the API endpoint to retrieve details about that superhero.

In OpenAPI, the documentation for such an endpoint would look like this:

```
openapi: 3.0.1
info:
  title: Example Superhero API
  version: "1.0"
servers:
- url: https://api.example.com/
paths:
  /superhero/{superhero_id}:
    get:
```

```
      parameters:
      - name: superhero_id
        in: path
        required: true
        schema:
          type: number
          format: int32
          enum:
          - 1
      responses:
        200:
          description: View a Superhero
          content:
            application/json:
              schema:
                $ref: '#/components/schemas/Superhero'
components:
  schemas:
    Superhero:
      title: Superhero
      type: object
      properties:
        name:
          type: string
        age:
          type: integer
          format: int32
        power:
          type: string
```

*Example 5.1: OpenAPI documentation for a superhero API*

The same function in RAML looks like this:

```
#%RAML 1.0
title: Example Superhero API
version: 1
baseUri: https://api.example.com/{version}
securitySchemes:
  digest:
    description: |
      This API supports DigestSecurityScheme
Authentication.
    type: Digest Authentication
/superhero/{id}:
  get:
    responses:
      200:
        body:
          application/json:
            type: Superhero
types:
  Superhero:
    type: object
    properties:
      name: string
      age: integer
      power: string
```

*Example 5.2: RAML documentation for a superhero API.*

Swagger can support YAML-style documentation that looks like this:

```
swagger: '2.0'
info:
  version: '1.0'
  title: Example Superhero API
host: api.example.com
basePath: /
schemes:
  - https
consumes:
  - application/json
produces:
  - application/json
paths:
  '/superhero/{superhero_id}':
    parameters:
      - name: superhero_id
        in: path
        required: true
        type: number
        format: int32
        enum:
          - 1
    get:
      responses:
        '200':
          description: View a Superhero
          schema:
            $ref: '#/definitions/Superhero'
definitions:
  Superhero:
    title: Superhero
```

```
type: object
properties:
  name:
    type: string
  age:
    type: integer
    format: int32
  power:
    type: string
```

*Example 5.3: Swagger/YAML documentation for a superhero API.*

Or JSON-style documentation like this:

```
{
  "swagger": "2.0",
  "info": {
    "version": "1.0",
    "title": "Example Superhero API"
  },
  "host": "api.example.com",
  "basePath": "/",
  "schemes": [
    "https"
  ],
  "consumes": [
    "application/json"
  ],
  "produces": [
    "application/json"
  ],
  "paths": {
    "/superhero/{superhero_id}": {
      "parameters": [
```

```
          {
            "name": "superhero_id",
            "in": "path",
            "required": true,
            "type": "number",
            "format": "int32",
            "enum": [
               1
            ]
          }
        ],
        "get": {
          "responses": {
            "200": {
              "description": "View a Superhero",
              "schema": {
                "$ref": "#/definitions/Superhero"
              }
            }
          }
        }
      }
    },
    "definitions": {
      "Superhero": {
        "title": "Superhero",
        "type": "object",
        "properties": {
          "name": {
            "type": "string"
          },
          "age": {
            "type": "integer",
```

```
        "format": "int32"
      },
      "power": {
        "type": "string"
      }
    }
  }
 }
}
```

*Example 5.4: Swagger/JSON documentation for a superhero API.*

The same function in BluePrint looks like this:

```
FORMAT: 1A
# Example Superhero API
## View a Superhero [/superhero/{superhero_id}]]
+ Response 200 (application/json)

    + Headers

        Location: /superhero/1

    + Body

        {
            "name": "Professor X",
            "age": "97",
            "power": "telepathy"
        }
```

*Example 5.5: BluePrint documentation for a superhero API.*

As there are several documentation languages for REST APIs, there are several tools to make these documentation types more readable. Apiary (apiary.io) and Swagger (swagger.io) will convert these documentation languages into easy-to-read web sites.

*Figure 5.3: Screen capture of OpenAPI code in the Apiary documentation viewer.*

## Tools to see REST API in action

A good way to understand, develop, and test REST APIs is to look at the raw requests and responses. This can be done with live or mock servers. A live server is useful for testing the integrity of the data but often costs money either to develop or in subscription fees. Mock data is useful for testing fake data or basic features and is often free.

Typically it does not store actual data and the responses are the same no matter what the request.

One way to implement a mock server is to create static text files with a .js file extension on a web server. Another is to use a pre-built mock server. REQ I RES is one such tool, which provides REST API endpoints for a variety of common use cases.

REQ I RES is available online at https://reqres.in/

Using REQ I RES, it is possible to preview the API payloads for several endpoints. These endpoints can also be accessed from client software such as a web application or mobile app or previewed online from the REQ I RES website. REQ I RES provides API endpoints for common functions for creating, reading, updating, and deleting data, as well as other common API functions such as registration, login, and a variety of possible error types.

*Figure 5.5: Screen capture of REQ I RES Mock API*

With REQ I RES and any programming language, it is possible to test a simple REST API Client. Since REST APIs are a standard across many programming languages, many developers know how to implement a client in their language, for instance, Python, JavaScript, Swift, Java, or PHP. Each of these languages has their own way of expressing the REST request and translating it into HTTP. HTTP is, therefore, the lingua franca of REST APIs and a lot of documentation focuses on describing the HTTP packet rather than a particular programming language implementation.

For example. Python may implement a request like this:

```
import requests
response = requests.get("https://reqres.in/api/users/2")
```

*Example 5.13: Python implementation of REST request*

Swift may implement a request like this:

```
var url : String = "https://reqres.in/api/users/2"
var request : NSMutableURLRequest =
NSMutableURLRequest()
request.URL = NSURL(string: url)
request.HTTPMethod = "GET"


NSURLConnection.sendAsynchronousRequest(request, queue:
NSOperationQueue(), completionHandler:
{ (response:NSURLResponse!, data: NSData!, error:
NSError!) -> Void in
    var error:
AutoreleasingUnsafeMutablePointer<NSError?> = nil
    let jsonResult: NSDictionary! =
NSJSONSerialization.JSONObjectWithData(data,
options:NSJSONReadingOptions.MutableContainers, error:
error) as? NSDictionary
    if (jsonResult != nil) {
        // process jsonResult
    } else {
        // couldn't load JSON, look at error
    }
})
```

*Example 5.14: Swift implementation of REST request*

The same API call in JavaScript is:

```
const userAction = async () => {
  const response = await fetch('https://reqres.in/api/
users/2');
  const myJson = await response.json(); //extract JSON
from the http response
  // do something with myJson
}
```

*Example 5.15: JavaScript implementation of REST request*

Each implementation is very different, but each essentially does the same thing:

1.  Build an HTTP Request

2.  Upload the request to a web server

3.  Download the server's response

Since each developer is expected to know their own language, documenting the REST API in plain HTTP is common:

```
GET /api/users/
Content-Type: application/json
```

*Example 5.16: HTTP implementation of REST request*

The resulting response would be something like the following:

```
200 OK
Content-Type: application/json; encoding=utf-8

{
```

```
"data": {
    "id": 2,
    "email": "janet.weaver@reqres.in",
    "first_name": "Janet",
    "last_name": "Weaver",
    "avatar": "https://s3.amazonaws.com/uifaces/
faces/twitter/josephstein/128.jpg"
    }
}
```

*Example 5.17: HTTP implementation of REST response*

This way, each developer knows how to use their language to build this request and how to process the resulting data.

# Conclusion

You now know how to find, learn, and work with REST APIs. Now it's time to work with existing REST APIs in your software or app, or to make your own. Good Luck!

# Glossary

**API:** Application Programming Interface - a set of functions and procedures allowing the creation of applications that access the features or data of an operating system, application, or other service.

**API Key:** An authentication credential for an API.

**Authorization Scheme:** A pre-defined mechanism for transmitting login credentials between a client and server over HTTP.

**Basic:** An authentication scheme that transmits an encoded login and password in the HTTP header.

**Bearer:** An authentication scheme that transmits a login session token in the HTTP header.

**Body:** The portion of a HTTP request or response that contains the representation of a resource.

**Caching:** The local storage of downloaded content to make access more efficient.

**CORS:** Cross Origin Resource Sharing - a mechanism that allows a web technology to access resources from domains other than the one it is being hosted on.

**Digest:** An authentication scheme that transmits an encoded api key in the HTTP header.

# Learn REST APIs

**Endpoint:** The unique address of a resource on a REST server.

**Header:** A portion of a HTTP request or response that contains information about the resource contained in the body or about the transmission of that resource.

**HTTP:** Hypertext Transfer Protocol - A protocol for sending data across the Internet

**Method:** The action to be taken on some resource, as defined by the HTTP protocol.

**OAuth:** An authentication scheme that transmits a login session token in the HTTP header.

**JSON:** JavaScript Object Notation - a way of representing resources using JavaScript's native syntax for describing data.

**Representation:** The use of a standard format to share a resource between two different computer systems.

**Request:** Data sent to a server by an HTTP client.

**Resource:** A package of data.

**Response**: Data sent to a client by an HTTP server.

**REST**: Representational State Transfer - A framework that defines how to communicate data between softwares on the Internet.

**URI:** A unique address accessible via the Internet

# Glossary

**Verb:** The action to be taken on some resource, as defined by the REST framework.

**XML:** eXtensible Markup Language - a markup language that can be used to create structured data using tags and text.

# Appendix I: HTTP Request Headers

| Name | Description | Example |
| --- | --- | --- |
| A-IM | Acceptable instance-manipulations for the request. | A-IM: feed |
| Accept | Media type(s) that is/are acceptable for the response. See Content negotiation. | Accept: text/html |
| Accept-Charset | Character sets that are acceptable. | Accept-Charset: utf-8 |
| Accept-Datetime | Acceptable version in time. | Accept-Datetime: Thu, 31 May 2007 20:35:00 GMT |
| Accept-Encoding | List of acceptable encodings. See HTTP compression. | Accept-Encoding: gzip, deflate |
| Accept-Language | List of acceptable human languages for response. See Content negotiation. | Accept-Language: en-US |
| Access-Control-Request-Method, Access-Control-Request-Headers | Initiates a request for cross-origin resource sharing with Origin(below). | Access-Control-Request-Method: GET |
| Authorization | Authentication credentials for HTTP authentication. | Authorization: Basic QWxhZGRpbjpvcGVuIHNlc2FtZQ== |
| Cache-Control | Used to specify directives that *must*be obeyed by all caching mechanisms along the request-response chain. | Cache-Control: no-cache |

| Name | Description | Example |
|---|---|---|
| Connection | Control options for the current connection and list of hop-by-hop request fields.<br><br>Must not be used with HTTP/2. | Connection: keep-alive<br><br>Connection: Upgrade |
| Content-Length | The length of the request body in octets (8-bit bytes). | Content-Length: 348 |
| Content-MD5 | A Base64-encoded binary MD5 sum of the content of the request body. | Content-MD5: Q2hlY2sgSW50ZWdyaXR5IQ== |
| Content-Type | The Media type of the body of the request (used with POST and PUT requests). | Content-Type: application/x-www-form-urlencoded |
| Cookie | An HTTP cookie previously sent by the server with Set-Cookie(below). | Cookie: $Version=1; Skin=new; |
| Date | The date and time at which the message was originated (in "HTTP-date" format as defined by RFC 7231 Date/Time Formats). | Date: Tue, 15 Nov 1994 08:12:31 GMT |
| Expect | Indicates that particular server behaviors are required by the client. | Expect: 100-continue |
| Forwarded | Disclose original information of a client connecting to a web server through an HTTP proxy. | Forwarded: for=192.0.2.60;proto=http;by=203.0.113.43Forwarded: for=192.0.2.43, for=198.51.100.17 |

# Appendix I: HTTP Request Headers

| Name | Description | Example |
|---|---|---|
| From | The email address of the user making the request. | From: user@example.com |
| Host | The domain name of the server (for virtual hosting), and the TCP port number on which the server is listening. The port number may be omitted if the port is the standard port for the service requested.<br><br>Mandatory since HTTP/1.1. If the request is generated directly in HTTP/2, it should not be used. | Host: en.wikipedia.org:8080<br><br>Host: en.wikipedia.org |
| HTTP2-Settings | A request that upgrades from HTTP/1.1 to HTTP/2 MUST include exactly one HTTP2-Settingheader field. The HTTP2-Settings header field is a connection-specific header field that includes parameters that govern the HTTP/2 connection, provided in anticipation of the server accepting the request to upgrade. | HTTP2-Settings: token64 |

| Name | Description | Example |
|---|---|---|
| If-Match | Only perform the action if the client supplied entity matches the same entity on the server. This is mainly for methods like PUT to only update a resource if it has not been modified since the user last updated it. | If-Match: "737060cd8c284d8af7ad308 2f209582d" |
| If-Modified-Since | Allows a *304 Not Modified* to be returned if content is unchanged. | If-Modified-Since: Sat, 29 Oct 1994 19:43:31 GMT |
| If-None-Match | Allows a *304 Not Modified* to be returned if content is unchanged, see HTTP ETag. | If-None-Match: "737060cd8c284d8af7ad308 2f209582d" |
| If-Range | If the entity is unchanged, send me the part(s) that I am missing; otherwise, send me the entire new entity. | If-Range: "737060cd8c284d8af7ad308 2f209582d" |
| If-Unmodified-Since | Only send the response if the entity has not been modified since a specific time. | If-Unmodified-Since: Sat, 29 Oct 1994 19:43:31 GMT |
| Max-Forwards | Limit the number of times the message can be forwarded through proxies or gateways. | Max-Forwards: 10 |

# Appendix I: HTTP Request Headers

| Name | Description | Example |
|------|-------------|---------|
| Origin | Initiates a request for cross-origin resource sharing (asks server for Access-Control-* response fields). | Origin: http://www.example-social-network.com |
| Pragma | Implementation-specific fields that may have various effects anywhere along the request-response chain. | Pragma: no-cache |
| Proxy-Authorization | Authorization credentials for connecting to a proxy. | Proxy-Authorization: Basic QWxhZGRpbjpvcGVuIHNl c2FtZQ== |
| Range | Request only part of an entity. Bytes are numbered from 0. See Byte serving. | Range: bytes=500-999 |
| Referer | This is the address of the previous web page from which a link to the currently requested page was followed. (The word "referrer" has been misspelled in the RFC as well as in most implementations to the point that it has become standard usage and is considered correct terminology) | Referer: http://en.wikipedia.org/wiki/Main_Page |

| Name | Description | Example |
|------|-------------|---------|
| TE | The transfer encodings the user agent is willing to accept: the same values as for the response header field Transfer-Encoding can be used, plus the "trailers" value (related to the "chunked" transfer method) to notify the server it expects to receive additional fields in the trailer after the last, zero-sized, chunk.<br>Only trailers is supported in HTTP/2. | TE: trailers, deflate |
| User-Agent | The user agent string of the user agent. | User-Agent: Mozilla/5.0 (X11; Linux x86_64; rv:12.0) Gecko/20100101 Firefox/12.0 |
| Upgrade | Ask the server to upgrade to another protocol.<br>Must not be used in HTTP/2. | Upgrade: h2c, HTTPS/1.3, IRC/6.9, RTA/x11, websocket |
| Via | Informs the server of proxies through which the request was sent. | Via: 1.0 fred, 1.1 example.com (Apache/1.1) |
| Warning | A general warning about possible problems with the entity body. | Warning: 199 Miscellaneous warning |

*Source: https://en.wikipedia.org/wiki/List_of_HTTP_header_fields*

# Appendix II: HTTP Response Headers

| Name | Description | Example |
|---|---|---|
| Access-Control-Allow-Origin, Access-Control-Allow-Credentials, Access-Control-Expose-Headers, Access-Control-Max-Age, Access-Control-Allow-Methods, Access-Control-Allow-Headers | Specifying which web sites can participate in cross-origin resource sharing | Access-Control-Allow-Origin: * |
| Accept-Patch | Specifies which patch document formats this server supports | Accept-Patch: text/example;charset=utf-8 |

| Name | Description | Example |
|---|---|---|
| Accept-Ranges | What partial content range types this server supports via byte serving | Accept-Ranges: bytes |
| Age | The age the object has been in a proxy cache in seconds | Age: 12 |
| Allow | Valid methods for a specified resource. To be used for a *405 Method not allowed* | Allow: GET, HEAD |
| Alt-Svc[44] | A server uses "Alt-Svc" header (meaning Alternative Services) to indicate that its resources can also be accessed at a different network location (host or port) or using a different protocol<br><br>When using HTTP/2, servers should instead send an ALTSVC frame. | Alt-Svc: http/1.1="http2.example.com:8001"; ma=7200 |
| Cache-Control | Tells all caching mechanisms from server to client whether they may cache this object. It is measured in seconds | Cache-Control: max-age=3600 |
| Connection | Control options for the current connection and list of hop-by-hop response fields.<br><br>Must not be used with HTTP/2. | Connection: close |
| Content-Disposition | An opportunity to raise a "File Download" dialogue box for a known MIME type with binary format or suggest a filename for dynamic content. Quotes are necessary with special characters. | Content-Disposition: attachment; filename="fname.ext" |

# Appendix II: HTTP Response Headers

| Name | Description | Example |
|------|-------------|---------|
| Content-Encoding | The type of encoding used on the data. See HTTP compression. | Content-Encoding: gzip |
| Content-Language | The natural language or languages of the intended audience for the enclosed content[47] | Content-Language: da |
| Content-Length | The length of the response body in octets (8-bit bytes) | Content-Length: 348 |
| Content-Location | An alternate location for the returned data | Content-Location: / index.htm |
| Content-MD5 | A Base64-encoded binary MD5 sum of the content of the response | Content-MD5: Q2hlY2sgSW50ZWdya XR5IQ== |
| Content-Range | Where in a full body message this partial message belongs | Content-Range: bytes 21010-47021 / 47022 |
| Content-Type | The MIME type of this content | Content-Type: text/ html; charset=utf-8 |
| Date | The date and time that the message was sent (in "HTTP-date" format as defined by RFC 7231) | Date: Tue, 15 Nov 1994 08:12:31 GMT |
| Delta-Base | Specifies the delta-encoding entity tag of the response. | Delta-Base: "abc" |
| ETag | An identifier for a specific version of a resource, often a message digest | ETag: "737060cd8c284d8af7ad 3082f209582d" |
| Expires | Gives the date / time after which the response is considered stale (in "HTTP-date" format as defined by RFC 7231) | Expires: Thu, 01 Dec 1994 16:00:00 GMT |
| IM | Instance-manipulations applied to the response. | IM: feed |

| Name | Description | Example |
|---|---|---|
| Last-Modified | The last modified date for the requested object (in "HTTP-date" format as defined by RFC 7231) | Last-Modified: Tue, 15 Nov 1994 12:45:26 GMT |
| Link | Used to express a typed relationship with another resource, where the relation type is defined by RFC 5988 | Link: </feed>; rel="alternate" |
| Location | Used in redirection, or when a new resource has been created. | • Example 1: Location: http://www.w3.org/pub/WWW/People.html<br><br>• Example 2: Location: /pub/WWW/People.html |
| P3P | This field is supposed to set P3P policy, in the form of P3P:CP="your_compact_policy". However, P3P did not take off, most browsers have never fully implemented it, a lot of websites set this field with fake policy text, that was enough to fool browsers the existence of P3P policy and grant permissions for third party cookies. | P3P: CP="This is not a P3P policy! See https://en.wikipedia.org/wiki/Special:CentralAutoLogin/P3P for more info." |
| Pragma | Implementation-specific fields that may have various effects anywhere along the request-response chain. | Pragma: no-cache |
| Proxy-Authenticate | Request authentication to access the proxy. | Proxy-Authenticate: Basic |

# Appendix II: HTTP Response Headers

| Name | Description | Example |
|------|-------------|---------|
| Public-Key-Pins[51] | HTTP Public Key Pinning, announces hash of website's authentic TLScertificate | Public-Key-Pins: max-age=2592000; pin-sha256="E9CZ9INDbd +2eRQozYqqbQ2yXLV KB9+xcprMF+44U1g="; |
| Retry-After | If an entity is temporarily unavailable, this instructs the client to try again later. Value could be a specified period of time (in seconds) or a HTTP-date. | • Example 1: Retry-After: 120<br><br>• Example 2: Retry-After: Fri, 07 Nov 2014 23:59:59 GMT |
| Server | A name for the server | Server: Apache/2.4.1 (Unix) |
| Set-Cookie | An HTTP cookie | Set-Cookie: UserID=JohnDoe; Max-Age=3600; Version=1 |
| Strict-Transport-Security | A HSTS Policy informing the HTTP client how long to cache the HTTPS only policy and whether this applies to subdomains. | Strict-Transport-Security: max-age=16070400; includeSubDomains |
| Trailer | The Trailer general field value indicates that the given set of header fields is present in the trailer of a message encoded with chunked transfer coding. | Trailer: Max-Forwards |
| Transfer-Encoding | The form of encoding used to safely transfer the entity to the user. Currently defined methods are: chunked, compress, deflate, gzip, identity.<br><br>Must not be used with HTTP/2. | Transfer-Encoding: chunked |

| Name | Description | Example |
|---|---|---|
| Tk | Tracking Status header, value suggested to be sent in response to a DNT(do-not-track), possible values:<br><br>"!" — under construction<br>"?" — dynamic<br>"G" — gateway to multiple parties<br>"N" — not tracking<br>"T" — tracking<br>"C" — tracking with consent<br>"P" — tracking only if consented<br>"D" — disregarding DNT<br>"U" — updated | Tk: ? |
| Upgrade | Ask the client to upgrade to another protocol.<br><br>Must not be used in HTTP/2 | Upgrade: h2c, HTTPS/1.3, IRC/6.9, RTA/x11, websocket |
| Vary | Tells downstream proxies how to match future request headers to decide whether the cached response can be used rather than requesting a fresh one from the origin server. | • Example 1: Vary: *<br><br>• Example 2: Vary: Accept-Language |
| Via | Informs the client of proxies through which the response was sent. | Via: 1.0 fred, 1.1 example.com (Apache/1.1) |
| Warning | A general warning about possible problems with the entity body. | Warning: 199 Miscellaneous warning |
| WWW-Authenticate | Indicates the authentication scheme that should be used to access the requested entity. | WWW-Authenticate: Basic |

Source: https://en.wikipedia.org/wiki/List_of_HTTP_header_fields

# Appendix III: HTTP Verbs

| Verb | HTTP Method |
|------|-------------|
| Create | POST |
| Read | GET |
| Update | PUT |
| Append | PATCH |
| Delete | DELETE |
| Endpoint Documentation | OPTIONS |
| Access HTTP Headers Only | HEAD |

# Appendix IV: HTTP Status Codes

## 1xx Informational

| Code | Meaning |
| --- | --- |
| 100 | Continue |
| 101 | Switching Protocols |
| 102 | Processing |

## 2xx Success

| Code | Meaning |
| --- | --- |
| 200 | OK |
| 201 | Created |
| 202 | Accepted |
| 203 | Non-authoritative Information |
| 204 | No Content |
| 205 | Reset Content |
| 206 | Partial Content |
| 207 | Multi-Status |
| 208 | Already Reported |
| 226 | IM Used |

## 3xx Redirection

| Code | Meaning |
| --- | --- |
| 300 | Multiple Choices |
| 301 | Moved Permanently |
| 302 | Found |
| 303 | See Other |
| 304 | Not Modified |
| 305 | Use Proxy |
| 307 | Temporary Redirect |
| 308 | Permanent Redirect |

## 4xx Client Error

| Code | Meaning |
| --- | --- |
| 400 | Bad Request |
| 401 | Unauthorized |
| 402 | Payment Required |
| 403 | Forbidden |
| 404 | Not Found |
| 405 | Method Not Allowed |
| 406 | Not Acceptable |

| | |
|---|---|
| 407 | Proxy Authentication Required |
| 408 | Request Timeout |
| 409 | Conflict |
| 410 | Gone |
| 411 | Length Required |
| 412 | Precondition Failed |
| 413 | Payload Too Large |
| 414 | Request-URI Too Long |
| 415 | Unsupported Media Type |
| 416 | Requested Range Not Satisfiable |
| 417 | Expectation Failed |
| 418 | I'm a teapot |
| 421 | Misdirected Request |
| 422 | Unprocessable Entity |
| 423 | Locked |
| 424 | Failed Dependency |
| 426 | Upgrade Required |
| 428 | Precondition Required |
| 429 | Too Many Requests |
| 431 | Request Header Fields Too Large |

| 444 | Connection Closed Without Response |
|-----|-----------------------------------|
| 451 | Unavailable For Legal Reasons |
| 499 | Client Closed Request |

## 5xx Server Error

| Code | Meaning |
|------|---------|
| 500 | Internal Server Error |
| 501 | Not Implemented |
| 502 | Bad Gateway |
| 503 | Service Unavailable |
| 504 | Gateway Timeout |
| 505 | HTTP Version Not Supported |
| 506 | Variant Also Negotiates |
| 507 | Insufficient Storage |
| 508 | Loop Detected |
| 510 | Not Extended |
| 511 | Network Authentication Required |
| 599 | Network Connect Timeout Error |

*Source: https://www.w3.org/Protocols/rfc2616/rfc2616-sec10.html*

# Appendix V: MIME-Types

| Extension | Document Type | MIME Type |
|---|---|---|
| .aac | AAC audio | audio/aac |
| .abw | AbiWord document | application/x-abiword |
| .arc | Archive document (multiple files embedded) | application/x-freearc |
| .avi | AVI: Audio Video Interleave | video/x-msvideo |
| .azw | Amazon Kindle eBook format | application/vnd.amazon.ebook |
| .bin | Any kind of binary data | application/octet-stream |
| .bmp | Windows OS/2 Bitmap Graphics | image/bmp |
| .bz | BZip archive | application/x-bzip |
| .bz2 | BZip2 archive | application/x-bzip2 |
| .csh | C-Shell script | application/x-csh |
| .css | Cascading Style Sheets (CSS) | text/css |
| .csv | Comma-separated values (CSV) | text/csv |
| .doc | Microsoft Word | application/msword |

| Extension | Document Type | MIME Type |
|---|---|---|
| .docx | Microsoft Word (OpenXML) | application/vnd.openxmlformats-officedocument.wordprocessingml.document |
| .eot | MS Embedded OpenType fonts | application/vnd.ms-fontobject |
| .epub | Electronic publication (EPUB) | application/epub+zip |
| .gif | Graphics Interchange Format (GIF) | image/gif |
| .htm<br>.html | HyperText Markup Language (HTML) | text/html |
| .ico | Icon format | image/vnd.microsoft.icon |
| .ics | iCalendar format | text/calendar |
| .jar | Java Archive (JAR) | application/java-archive |
| .jpeg<br>.jpg | JPEG images | image/jpeg |
| .js | JavaScript | text/javascript |
| .json | JSON format | application/json |
| .jsonld | JSON-LD format | application/ld+json |
| .mid<br>.midi | Musical Instrument Digital Interface (MIDI) | audio/midi audio/x-midi |

# Appendix V: MIME-Types

| Extension | Document Type | MIME Type |
|---|---|---|
| .mjs | JavaScript module | text/javascript |
| .mp3 | MP3 audio | audio/mpeg |
| .mpeg | MPEG Video | video/mpeg |
| .mpkg | Apple Installer Package | application/vnd.apple.installer+xml |
| .odp | OpenDocument presentation document | application/vnd.oasis.opendocument.presentation |
| .ods | OpenDocument spreadsheet document | application/vnd.oasis.opendocument.spreadsheet |
| .odt | OpenDocument text document | application/vnd.oasis.opendocument.text |
| .oga | OGG audio | audio/ogg |
| .ogv | OGG video | video/ogg |
| .ogx | OGG | application/ogg |
| .otf | OpenType font | font/otf |
| .png | Portable Network Graphics | image/png |
| .pdf | Adobe Portable Document Format(PDF) | application/pdf |
| .ppt | Microsoft PowerPoint | application/vnd.ms-powerpoint |

| Extension | Document Type | MIME Type |
| --- | --- | --- |
| .pptx | Microsoft PowerPoint (OpenXML) | application/vnd.openxmlformats-officedocument.presentationml.presentation |
| .rar | RAR archive | application/x-rar-compressed |
| .rtf | Rich Text Format (RTF) | application/rtf |
| .sh | Bourne shell script | application/x-sh |
| .svg | Scalable Vector Graphics (SVG) | image/svg+xml |
| .swf | Small web format (SWF) or Adobe Flash document | application/x-shockwave-flash |
| .tar | Tape Archive (TAR) | application/x-tar |
| .tif .tiff | Tagged Image File Format (TIFF) | image/tiff |
| .ts | MPEG transport stream | video/mp2t |
| .ttf | TrueType Font | font/ttf |
| .txt | Text, (generally ASCII or ISO 8859-$n$) | text/plain |
| .vsd | Microsoft Visio | application/vnd.visio |
| .wav | Waveform Audio Format | audio/wav |
| .weba | WEBM audio | audio/webm |
| .webm | WEBM video | video/webm |

# Appendix V: MIME-Types

| Extension | Document Type | MIME Type |
|---|---|---|
| .webp | WEBP image | image/webp |
| .woff | Web Open Font Format (WOFF) | font/woff |
| .woff2 | Web Open Font Format (WOFF) | font/woff2 |
| .xhtml | XHTML | application/xhtml+xml |
| .xls | Microsoft Excel | application/vnd.ms-excel |
| .xlsx | Microsoft Excel (OpenXML) | application/vnd.openxmlformats-officedocument.spreadsheetml.sheet |
| .xml | XML | application/xml if *not* readable from casual users (RFC 3023, section 3)<br><br>text/xml if readable from casual users (RFC 3023, section 3) |
| .xul | XUL | application/vnd.mozilla.xul+xml |
| .zip | ZIP archive | application/zip |
| .3gp | 3GPP audio/video container | video/3gpp<br><br>audio/3gpp if it doesn't contain video |
| .3g2 | 3GPP2 audio/video container | video/3gpp2<br><br>audio/3gpp2 if it doesn't contain video |

| Extension | Document Type | MIME Type |
|---|---|---|
| .7z | 7-zip archive | application/x-7z-compressed |

*Source: http://www.iana.org/assignments/media-types/media-types.xhtml*

# About the Author

 Tony's infinite curiosity compels him to want to open up and learn about everything he touches, and his excitement compels him to share what he learns with others.

He has two true passions: branding and inventing.

His passion for branding led him to start a company that did branding and marketing in 4 countries for firms such as Apple, Intel, and Sony BMG. He loves weaving the elements of design, writing, product, and strategy into an essential truth that defines a company.

His passion for inventing led him to start a company that uses brain imaging to quantify meditation and to predict seizures, which acquired $1.5m in funding and was incubated in San Francisco where he currently resides.

Those same passions have led him on some adventures as well, including living in a Greek monastery with orthodox monks and to tagging along with a busker in Spain to learn how to play flamenco guitar.

# About this Book

The Internet runs on REST APIs. Social media apps, hotel, and travel sites, Netflix, and more use APIs to load, save, and analyze data over the Internet.

REST APIs are built to be used by 3rd party products such as mobile apps and other web sites. They enable companies to create new revenue streams by creating a white-label product that others resell and attract new customers.

This book will teach you what REST APIs are, why they are useful, and how to use them to build more scalable, faster, more efficient applications. In this book, you will learn:

- What is a REST API

- How are REST APIs used

- Why are REST APIs useful

- How REST works with HTTP

- Anatomy of a REST Request and Response

- Best Practices

- How to create, read, update, and delete data

- Where to find REST APIs